THE HOPPERS
LIMESTONE TRAFFIC

Paul Harrison

AMBERLEY

First published 2020

Amberley Publishing
The Hill, Stroud
Gloucestershire, GL5 4EP

www.amberley-books.com

Copyright © Paul Harrison, 2020

The right of Paul Harrison to be identified as
the Author of this work has been asserted in
accordance with the Copyrights, Designs and
Patents Act 1988.

ISBN 978 1 4456 9528 0 (print)
ISBN 978 1 4456 9529 7 (ebook)

British Library Cataloguing in Publication Data.
A catalogue record for this book is available from
the British Library.

Origination by Amberley Publishing.
Printed in the UK.

Introduction

For over eighty-four years block trainloads of hopper wagons have been conveying crushed limestone from the vast Tunstead quarry, near Buxton, Derbyshire, to the soda ash and chemicals plants at Northwich, Cheshire. The initial design for a high-capacity bogie hopper wagon came about from the increased demand for soda ash in the 1930s, and thus the raw limestone needed for the Solvay chemical process. To understand how the hopper trains came about it is useful to have a short history and chemistry lesson.

By the late 1860s the main railway lines linking Derbyshire, Lancashire and Cheshire were complete, allowing limestone to be transported by rail to works in Widnes. Chemist Ludwig Mond and industrialist John Brunner established their soda ash plant at Winnington, in Northwich, in October 1873, and, by April 1874, were starting to produce sodium bicarbonate, via the Solvay ammonia-soda chemical process, using limestone quarried from the Peak Forest area. In 1900, Brunner, Mond & Co. Ltd acquired the nearby works of Bowman, Thompson & Co. Ltd, at Lostock Gralam, which, after reconstruction, resumed ammonia-soda production in 1907. By 1919, Brunner, Mond had acquired the Buxton Lime Firms Ltd Company, thus securing the important flow of limestone. Brunner, Mond was one of the four main companies that merged in 1926 to form Imperial Chemical Industries (I. C. I.); the other three companies were the British Dyestuffs Corporation, Nobel's Explosives Limited, and the United Alkali Company. The Brunner, Mond part of I. C. I. business soon became part of the Alkali Group.

The Solvay ammonia-soda chemical process can be summarised as follows:

A solution of concentrated brine is extracted from the vast salt beds beneath Northwich and the nearby Cheshire plain. The Sodium chloride brine is firstly "purified" by having Calcium and Magnesium salts removed before being passed through two towers; the first introduces Ammonia which is absorbed by the brine. In the second tower, Carbon dioxide is introduced to the ammoniated brine and Sodium bicarbonate is precipitated out. The Carbon dioxide required for the reaction is produced by the heating or 'calcination' of high-purity Derbyshire limestone at high temperatures by burning coke. The Calcium carbonate is converted to become quick lime (Calcium oxide) and Carbon dioxide. The Sodium bicarbonate and the Ammonium chloride liquor are separated. The Ammonium chloride is reacted with slaked lime (generated by adding water to the quick lime in what are called "dissolvers"). The reaction between the slaked lime and the Ammonium chloride releases free Ammonia, which is recycled back to the initial brine reaction stage. And so, Sodium bicarbonate is then converted to the final product, Sodium carbonate, by a thermal decomposition reaction at temperatures of about 165 degrees Celsius. This reaction produces water and Carbon dioxide, both of which can be re-used again. Therefore, the main ingredients for the Solvay process are salt and limestone with thermal energy provided from coke and steam.

With the creation of I. C. I. in 1926, thoughts turned to how the increased demand for soda ash could be met. The construction of a new works at Wallerscote, just across the road from Winnington, commenced prior to the First World War, and eventually opened in 1926. To help with demand, plans were made by I. C. I. to tap into new reserves of limestone at Tunstead. Whether it was foresight or forward planning, I. C. I. took the decision to develop the quarry at Tunstead in order to rapidly increase the output of limestone and related products. The new quarry was developed at Tunstead from 1927, just to the south of Great Rocks, and opened fully in 1929. This would later go on to become the longest worked quarry face, a mile and a quarter in length. The limestone comes from Carboniferous era Chee Tor formation, some 300 million years old. This limestone is the high-purity stone needed at Northwich some 25 miles away to the west. The lower purity Woo Dale limestone would later be used for aggregate and construction purposes. Tunstead quarry is now owned and operated by Tarmac, a CRH company.

The existing fleet of two-axle wooden open wagons was inherited from Brunner Mond and the former Buxton Lime Firms companies and were of varying designs and capacities. These had been in use from the 1860s onwards. Manual loading and unloading of these wagons was very time consuming at both ends. Ideally, a more efficient fleet of wagons was needed to permit better loading and unloading facilities and, thus, better quarry facilities too.

After some initial design ideas and meetings in 1931 between I. C. I., the railway companies and authorities, it was agreed during 1934 that a bogie hopper wagon design would be suitable. During February 1935, trials took place using a pair of LNER bogie open sulphate wagons of a similar length and wheelbase. The wagons were used to test the clearances around the three main works at Northwich, where the proposed wagons would operate. They were also tried at Middlewich works but the tight track curves caused problems and so plans to use the hoppers there were halted. The recommendation for the Northwich traffic was to place an order for 40-ton bogie hopper wagons to a design developed with the acclaimed railway rolling stock builder Charles Roberts & Co. of Wakefield. For the Middlewich traffic, a new fleet of five-plank open wagons was ordered, in 1937, from the Gloucester Railway Carriage & Wagon Co.

The initial order for three wagons was placed in April 1936 and they were delivered by December of that year from Charles Roberts & Co. to Imperial Chemical Industries Alkali Division, at Tunstead. After initial trials of the wagons in late 1936 and 1937 the wagons were accepted, and production resumed at Wakefield. A proposal to use the LMS Garratt 2-6-0 + 0-6-2 heavy-freight locomotives was put forward by I. C. I., with assistance from the LMS, in a report dated July 1936, but this plan never came to fruition. A detailed report produced by I. C. I. explained how the services would operate using two Garratt locomotives hauling sixteen wagons, each working two return trips between Tunstead and Winnington per day. Any excess tonnage would be moved using a Class 4F locomotive. In the event, the first train of eleven loaded wagons, plus a brake van, set off from Tunstead on 4 October

1937, hauled by an LMS Class 4F with a Class 4F pilot assisting on the front, to Peak Forest.

After the first run the trains of hoppers continued operating with Class 4F engines, hauling a maximum of eleven loaded wagons. Trains of loaded wagons and the return empties ran via Chinley, New Mills, Cheadle Heath, Altrincham and Knutsford. However, if the booked route, via Disley Tunnel, was blocked, then the diversionary route was via Romiley and Stockport Tiviot Dale with a reduced load of only nine loaded wagons plus a brake van.

On 1 December 1938, LMS Class 8F No. 8026 successfully took a loaded rake of seventeen hoppers, plus a brake van, from Tunstead to Northwich. Again, from Tunstead sidings to Peak Forest, assistance was provided by a Class 4F pilot. Class 8F locomotives became the primary traction for the hopper train until the mid-1960s. The 8Fs were booked to haul rakes of sixteen wagons to and from Northwich and engines for this traffic were initially based at Heaton Mersey shed. The wagon fleet gradually built up to eighty-four, which had all been delivered by the end of 1939. During the years of the Second World War, the hopper trains continued to operate daily and, given the wartime restrictions, photos of the hopper trains during this period are rare.

After the Second World War, I. C. I. ordered another batch of thirty-six wagons from Charles Roberts in August 1945 and these were built and delivered thereafter. By around April 1949, most of the hopper traffic was being worked by Class 8Fs and crews based at Northwich shed. A final batch of thirty-two wagons was ordered in June 1951 onwards, with the last wagons being delivered in 1953. This brought the total number of these hopper wagons owned by I. C. I. to 152. The only alteration made to the hoppers was the fitting of roller bearings to the bogies from 1966 onwards.

Charles Roberts had also started construction of a batch of similar unfitted wagons for John Summers & Sons in 1951. These wagons were used solely on the flow of imported iron ore from Bidston Docks, near Birkenhead, to the steel works at Shotton, located at the south end of the Wirral peninsula. These heavy eleven-wagon trains utilised Class 9F heavy freight locomotives from 1953 onwards. Sometimes Class 8Fs were used with only nine wagons. From November 1967 onwards, diesel locomotives, often Brush Type 4s (later Class 47s), were used. This traffic ceased in 1980, when pairs of Class 24s or 25s moved the iron ore, as steelmaking at the British Steel Corporation Shotton works had come to an end. The works switched to become a finishing and coatings plant. Today, Shotton Works is part of the Tata Steel group.

Diesels started to take over the I. C. I. hopper traffic from the early 1960s after extensive trials. The first trials used Metro-Vick 'Co-Bos' Type 2s and then English Electric '1-Co-Co-1' Type 4s (later Class 40s) on the Northwich traffic during 1963. Eventually the I. C. I. services used new Derby-built Type 2s (Class 25s) with one additional Darlington-built loco added to the fleet. The Type 2s started in August 1964 and remained on the hopper flows until around 1984. In 1968, a new roadstone traffic flow started from Tunstead, utilising the hopper wagons, and twenty-three spare wagons were initially pooled for aggregates services for Quickmix Concrete Co. The limestone was extracted from the lower grade Woo Dale strata – still of good quality for general aggregates and construction use. Initially, the 'Road Stone' branded wagons worked to a new terminal at Dean Lane, opposite the British Railways Newton Heath diesel depot. Later, additional receiving terminals were established at Collyhurst Street, near Miles Platting, Pendleton, and the former Portwood coal drops near Stockport Tiviot Dale station. Trains of twelve loaded hopper wagons operated to serve the terminals either daily or as required. For a short period in the early 1970s the hoppers operated to a Tarmac stone terminal at Carterhouse Lane, in Widnes. Once Tarmac had taken delivery of new two-axle air-braked hopper wagons the flow changed over to use these wagons instead.

Class 25s worked the trains, assisted as required by the Class 40s and later Class 47s, on the main Mond services to Northwich and the roadstone traffic. In 1972, the hopper wagons were given a new number range with the introduction of the British Railways Total Operations Processing System, or TOPS as it was known. The original fleet numbers up until then were Nos 3200 to 3351. They were gradually renumbered in order to Nos 19000 to 19151 and given the owner code ICIM, meaning I. C. I. Mond Division, Northwich. The wagons were coded PHV – Private Owner Hopper, bogie, vacuum-braked. By around 1980, Class 37s and 45s were making appearances on the roadstone services and operated singly at this time.

Up until 1982, I. C. I. had lost thirteen of its hopper wagons to accident damage, caused mainly by derailments and mishaps. As you will see in the photographs the hopper wagons had had their fair share of mishaps, some minor and three major accidents where the wagons were totally written off.

Fortuitously, the Shotton iron ore hopper fleet was now redundant and most of these PHO type wagons were laid up in Shotwick sidings. It is believed that British Rail initially decided to purchase eight of these wagons by way of compensation to I. C. I. The eight wagons were moved to Northwich and given a full overhaul at I. C. I.'s Avenue engineering workshops. This involved fitting vacuum brake equipment and roller bearings to the bogies. A large quantity of spares, mainly pairs of bogies from the British Steel Corporation fleet, was also purchased by I. C. I. This would allow I. C. I. to fit the plate frame bogies to the first eighty-four wagons, which were running on original diamond frame bogies. This had the benefit of all the I. C. I. fleet being fitted with the same bogies with roller bearings and able to convey the same forty-seven tons of stone. An additional five wagons were purchased and overhauled in the same manner to bring the fleet back to 152 wagons. The 'new' wagons were added to the existing roadstone pool.

With the availability of Class 25 and 40 locomotives being reduced due to withdrawals, BR decided to trial a pair of Class 20s in September 1982. The Class 20 pair successfully hauled twenty-four loaded wagons to Northwich and by all accounts it was considered a success. Following this, the class were introduced onto the hopper services from May 1984 onwards, working alongside the Class 37s, 45s and 47s as required. In late 1985, a decision was made to experimentally fit air brake equipment to the first I. C. I. wagon, No. ICIM 19000, at Avenue works. The exact outcome and how they tested the wagon isn't clear – it seems the trials lasted for the first half of 1986, after which the air brake equipment was removed, and the wagon became a PHV once more. In April 1986, another scheme saw eight of the Class 20s converted to a new sub-Class 20/3, fitted with modified braking equipment for use with the PHV wagons. The eight locomotives, Nos 20301 to 20308, lasted in this guise for about a year before the experiment was abandoned and the locomotives renumbered back to their original identities. A pair of newly refurbished Class 37/7s, Nos 37796 and 37803, were sent to Buxton from Crewe works in December 1986. They were successfully used on the Northwich flows as a pair and singly too. As a result, Buxton depot received its own fleet of thirteen refurbished Class 37/5 locomotives from Spring 1987 onwards. Officially, these were allocated to Tinsley depot, near Sheffield.

A new flow of limestone, using some of the roadstone wagons, started in 1987 between Tunstead and Hindlow. The I. C. I. quarry and lime processing plant at Hindlow had ceased quarrying and so it was decided to source the limestone from nearby Tunstead. Class 37s remained the preferred traction on the Hindlow services until around 1993, though Class 20s were used too. Pairs of Class 31s were often used on the roadstone flows and occasionally were used on the Mond traffic, especially when diverted via Buxton. Class 47s tended to stick to the Mond traffic, and these were often freight-only Class 47/0s and ex-passenger Class 47/4s. With a downturn in the construction industry, some of the roadstone services ceased in 1990. Surplus wagons from this pool were re-used for the Hindlow traffic. In 1991, the I. C. I. empire was broken up and divested into a series of smaller companies. The quarries at Tunstead and Hindlow became Buxton Lime Industries (B. L. I.) and the two soda ash plants at Northwich went to Brunner Mond Ltd. However, the re-coded JGV wagons became the property of B. L. I. The traffic to Northwich and Hindlow continued as before but, from 1993 onwards, the vacuum-braked hoppers were replaced by more modern air-braked wagons on the Hindlow workings.

From this point the original wagon fleet was gradually reduced and some wagons found use internally at the Northwich works. For a short time, in July 1995, a rake of 'Dogfish' ballast hopper wagons were used with the JGV wagons to make up the shortfall in the fleet. These were hired in from Transrail and used with the JGV hoppers and separately in a single rake. As the age and the limited capacity were ever apparent, it was decided to withdraw the wagons by the end of 1997. During the late 1990s, several schemes were put forward to modernise the old hopper wagons by fitting air brakes and new bogies, but nothing came of the plans.

The last loaded service formed of the veteran JGV hoppers ran on 28 December 1997, with a return empty train running two days later on 30 December. After this, trains started to use the 1970s-built two-axle air-braked PGA hopper wagons, formerly operated by ARC and Foster Yeoman, in the Mendips area. These wagons were hired from wagon leaser CAIB and, towards the end of 1997, by Brunner Mond. The first loaded trial train of PGAs ran on 21 November 1997. The rather worn rag-tag fleet of seemingly multi-coloured wagons took over and were often loaded to thirty-six wagons, initially powered by Class 60s, but, for a time, pairs of Class 37s took over again. Other EWS locomotives, including the Class 59/2 locomotives, were used and on at least one occasion a Class 56 too. In July 1999, and again at Christmas that year, the freight train operator EWS decided to trial a rake of the then new MBA 102-tonne bogie open box wagons. Quite why this happened is not known as these wagons have no bottom-discharge doors, and so the limestone would need to be removed using a grab bucket. The wagons spent some time at Lostock and Winnington until, eventually, the stone was unloaded, but by then it was of little use to Brunner Mond.

The remaining JGV hopper wagons were laid up at Tunstead, Lostock and Winnington works pending a decision. Brunner Mond was still using the wagons internally, at both the Lostock and Winnington works, to move stockpiled limestone and coke around the works. In June 1998, a rake of thirty-six wagons were dispatched for scrap by rail from Tunstead to the EMR scrapyard at Attercliffe, Sheffield. Further wagons were sent from Northwich to EMR, at Salford, for scrapping at the end of 1999. Brunner Mond successfully received a Freight Facilities Grant from the Government towards the cost of purchasing new wagons from W. H. Davis and updating the discharging facilities at Northwich. The new facilities were commissioned in late 2000 with a trial load of thirteen new wagons on 15 November 2000. After the last trainload of the PGA hoppers, on 30 December 2000, the traffic went over to the new 76-tonne payload JEA bogie hopper wagons on 1 January 2001. The PGA fleet went off-lease, and some were stored near Grimsby pending re-use or scrapping.

These JEA hoppers were built by W. H. Davis of Shirebrook to a joint design with Brunner Mond and, at the time of writing, have been in traffic for just over eighteen years now. Apart from some essential repair work that grounded the JEA fleet in 2007, these hoppers have carried on with the job. Whilst being repaired they were replaced by hired-in Freightliner HIA bogie hoppers hauled by EWS Class 60s. Sadly, the flow of limestone to Winnington ceased in 2014 when the decision was made by Tata Chemicals Europe to stop the production of soda ash on site. And so, this left Lostock as the sole soda ash plant in Northwich. In a surprise move the JEA hopper wagons were sold by Tata Chemicals Europe to DB Schenker in 2015. Apart from routine maintenance on the running gear, the wagons retain their much faded and worn grey Brunner Mond livery and logos.

Only more recently, when DB Cargo was short of drivers at Peak Forest, did the traffic have a change of operator and wagons. This time Freightliner Heavy Haul stepped in to cover the flow to Lostock using its own Class 66/6 locomotives and the 90-tonne capacity HIA hopper wagons. The JEA fleet soon found gainful employment, bringing trainloads of glass cullet from Tilbury, East London to the Encirc glassworks at Ince & Elton. In June 2018, DB Cargo took the traffic back over and re-instated the JEA fleet. The train diagram was amended to start and end at Warrington Arpley. Empty wagons would be taken to Tunstead sidings in the morning; the Class 60 would run light to stable at Peak Forest whilst the JEAs were loaded up. In the afternoon the twenty-four-wagon train departs Tunstead for Lostock works, where the hoppers are discharged. Late in the evening, the empties run to Arpley yard where the train stables overnight. The three spare JEA wagons are kept at Arpley yard and swapped over as required for maintenance.

Six of the former I. C. I. PHV hopper wagons survived into preservation. The remaining six wagons that had been stored at Tunstead lasted until the autumn of 2012, when they were finally cut-up on site following several aborted preservation attempts. 'The Hoppers' will keep on rolling up and down the lines from Tunstead to Lostock for some time yet – possibly until the mid-2040s when it is estimated that the limestone reserves at Tunstead will be exhausted.

Thanks go to my partner, Claire, my parents, Pam & Colin, my brother, Steven, and Uncle Stanley for their encouragement to do this book. Thanks to all those who have helped with photograph contributions to the book – it is amazing how many new images of the hoppers I have discovered in the past decade. I hope that you enjoy the photographs that I have selected. I spent many hours looking through the various collections to select suitable photos to include and writing up the captions and information from my notes.

If you have enjoyed this book, then you may be interested in a DVD entitled *The Hoppers – Moving Derbyshire into Cheshire*, produced by Railfilms Ltd. and available online from www.telerail.co.uk.

Paul Harrison
Hazel Grove
September 2019

This is where the story of 'The Hoppers' starts, with this wagon, No. 3200, shown here shortly after delivery to I. C. I. and seen in the works sidings at Tunstead, having drawn the attention of the works photographer. Taken on 3 December 1936. (Courtesy of Tarmac Buxton Cement & Lime)

Second-built wagon No. 3201, also seen at Tunstead. It is identical to No. 3200 except for the hand-brake lever replacing the hand-brake wheel. Note also the small LTD letters fitted alongside the I letter. Only the first three wagons received this and it remained on the wagons until at least the mid-1960s. Taken on 3 December 1936. (Courtesy of Tarmac Buxton Cement & Lime)

The final wagon of the initial trio of wagons at Tunstead was No. 3202. From this angle it is hard to tell whether the wagons are loaded, however history shows that the wagons operated from Tunstead to Winnington and Lostock works on trial, pending delivery of the production wagons. Taken on 3 December 1936. (Courtesy of Tarmac Buxton Cement & Lime)

With railway and quarry officials lined up alongside the locomotive crew, this is thought to be the occasion of the first trainload of eleven loaded I. C. I. hopper wagons, waiting to leave Tunstead. The train engine is an LMS (London, Midland & Scottish Railway) Class 4F with a further Class 4F, acting as pilot engine, for the steep climb up to the summit at Peak Forest. Taken on 4 October 1937. (Courtesy of Tarmac Buxton Cement & Lime)

LMS No. 3881 drifts along the Down slow line and past Gowhole marshalling yard. The locomotive had eleven loaded hoppers behind, plus an LMS brake van. The train will soon cross over to take the direct line to Cheadle Heath, via Disley Tunnel. Taken on 4 June 1938. (R. D. Pollard/Manchester Locomotive Society (MLS) collection)

Just over fourteen months after the first train of eleven wagons another milestone took place when the LMS trialled one of its Class 8F 2-8-0 heavy-freight locomotives on the hopper trains. No. 8026 is seen at the head of the first train of seventeen loaded wagons, at Tunstead, with brake van, again piloted by a Class 4F. Taken on 2 December 1938. (Courtesy of Tarmac Buxton Cement & Lime)

A superb view, from high up on the hillside at Tunstead, looking down on the first Class 8F-hauled train of hoppers, this time from the other end of the yard. A variety of wooden open wagons, some with sheeted loads, and the newer hopper wagons are dotted around the yard. Taken on 2 December 1938. (Courtesy of Tarmac Buxton Cement & Lime)

No. 8017 is seen rounding the curve linking Skelton Junction to Deansgate Junction, near Timperley, with the yard and original turntable in the foreground. From here the hopper trains had to be given a clear run through to Hale station to climb up the short and curved Hale Bank. Taken during April 1939 (W. Potter/MLS collection)

Under clear signals, No. 8087 rolls down from Peak Forest and has just cleared Chapel-en-le-Frith Central station with a load of hoppers. On each side of the main Up and Down lines are the goods loops. Taken on 30 May 1939. (R. D. Pollard/MLS collection)

Passing under Manchester Road overbridge and through the former Cheshire Lines Committee (CLC) station at Cheadle, we see No. 8089 with a loaded rake of hoppers for Northwich. The station building, seen to the right, survives to this day as the Cheshire Line Tavern public house and restaurant. Taken during June 1939. (W. Potter/MLS collection)

The hopper trains continued to operate throughout the Second World War years and here we see No. 8220 in the final months of LMS operation, before Nationalisation took place on 1 January 1948. The empty hopper train has just passed New Mills South Junction and under Marsh Lane overbridge, seen in the background. Taken on 21 June 1947. (MLS collection)

As a rule, the hopper trains were booked to run on the fast lines between Chinley North and New Mills South Junctions, but on occasion they were crossed over on to the slow lines instead. No. 8697 is about to pass under Dakin's bridge, Chinley, with loaded hoppers for Northwich on the Down slow line. Taken on 30 August 1947. (MLS collection)

LMS No. 8220 is seen passing through Chapel-en-le-Frith with Up empty hoppers, with the Down and Up loops alongside the main lines. The Up loop was often host to two freight trains that would need to recess out of the way of express passenger trains and wait their turn to climb the last few miles to Peak Forest. Taken on 27 September 1947. (MLS collection)

Wagon No. 3215 is seen stabled in sidings, believed to be Oakleigh sidings at Northwich, pending departure back to Great Rocks sidings for Tunstead, where it will collect another load of limestone. The bogie wagon design could be considered a revolution when first introduced in 1936, and they moved limestone day in, day out solidly until 1997. Taken *c.* 1948. (Author's collection)

In 1948 Tunstead Quarry took part in the Quarrying with Safety Exhibition and here we see wagon No. 3200 at the head of a rake of loaded hoppers. The man is showing how the handbrakes are applied to the wagons to pin the brakes down before the steam shunting engine arrives to couple up to the train and move them away. Taken on 27 October 1948. (Courtesy of Tarmac Buxton Cement & Lime)

A classic view of the junction at Chinley North as No. 8697, with empty hoppers, passes over the crossing and points forming the connection to the slow lines. The four-track line divides here into double-track routes to Derby, via Peak Forest, and Dore, via the Hope Valley. Taken on 8 May 1948. (J. D. Darby/MLS collection)

Having just passed the marshalling yard at Gowhole, just to the east of New Mills, No. 8154 will soon pass New Mills South Junction and take the former Midland Railway cut-off line via Disley Tunnel; the line was opened in 1902. Taken on 15 May 1948. (MLS collection)

Under clear signals, Class 8F No. 8316 has just passed through the station at Chapel-en-le-Frith Central on the Down line. The former Midland Railway station was much better sited than the rival LNWR station, which is nearly a mile away to the south on the hillside. It has been suggested that Chapel regains its station here to tap into the commuter routes towards Manchester. Taken on 12 June 1948. (MLS collection)

The engine crew of No. 8190 will either be heartened or dismayed by seeing the signal routing them into the Up loop at Chapel-en-le-Frith. Watched by a fellow enthusiast, the train of empty hoppers passes over Chapel Milton viaduct and over Chinley South Junction. Taken on 11 September 1948. (J. D. Darby/MLS collection)

Skirting through the countryside to the south of Stockport, near Bridge Hall, Adswood, is No. 8190 with a rake of empty hoppers for Great Rocks. In the background you can see a train of goods vans and opens on the LNWR line embankment. The footbridge here still exists but the line is now singled, and the skyline occupied by light industrial units, a police station and new houses. Taken c. 1948. (MLS collection)

After Nationalisation the Class 8F locomotives were renumbered from the LMS 8xxx series to the BR 48xxx series. Here we see No. 48154 passing through Northenden station with empties for Great Rocks sidings. Class 8Fs were the main locomotives used on the hopper trains between December 1936 and August 1964, when the diesel-electric locomotives took over with the occasional steam substitution. Taken on 9 May 1949. (A. C. Gilbert/MLS collection)

Looking from the footbridge at the west end of Chinley station, we see No. 48099 crossing over from the Down slow line to the Down fast with a loaded train of hoppers. In the background, above the locomotive, is Chinley Station North Junction signalbox. Taken on 23 July 1949. (MLS collection)

Exiting the 2-mile, 346-yard Disley Tunnel in spectacular fashion is No. 48220, with a train of empty hoppers for Great Rocks sidings. The eastern portal structure is a much grander design than the western portal and incorporates the Midland Railway wyvern motif in the stonework above the tracks. Taken on 4 September 1949. (W. D. Cooper/ Gordon Coltas Photographic Trust)

The bobby in Chinley South Junction signalbox has given the engine crew of No. 48154 a caution aspect with the old Midland Railway lower quadrant semaphore signals. Milepost 168 is in the foreground in this view from Stoddard's overbridge. Taken on 3 June 1950. (R. D. Pollard/MLS collection)

No. 48406 makes steady progress along the Up fast line, near Buxworth, on its way towards Chinley and the summit at Peak Forest with just ten hoppers and a brake van in tow. By now British Railways had made its mark on many of the Class 8F locomotives, though some still escaped works attention of course. Taken on 1 July 1950. (MLS collection)

The standard load for a Class 8F was sixteen wagons and, on occasion, seventeen wagons with a brake van attached to the rear. Any additional empty wagons were often returned to Great Rocks in the head of other goods trains heading back towards Peak Forest, where the wagons could be detached and tripped the short distance to the reception sidings. No. 48676 is seen hauling one such train near New Mills South Junction. Taken on 19 August 1950. (R. D. Pollard/MLS collection)

The route of the hopper trains on the former Midland Railway lines curves around the west side of Chapel-en-le-Frith and then heads directly towards the Cowlow hillside, to the south-east, into Dove Holes tunnel. No. 48503 passes through Chapel with a rake of empty hoppers for Great Rocks sidings. Taken during October 1950. (W. D. Cooper/Gordon Coltas Photographic Trust)

Climbing steadily up the 1 in 132 gradient towards Disley Tunnel, near Hazel Grove, is No. 48680, heading back to Tunstead. The New Mills & Heaton Mersey Line opened in 1902 and is still in use today as a passenger and freight line as far as Hazel Grove High Level Junction, thence freight-only single line to Cheadle Heath, then the former CLC line to Northenden. Taken on 1 March 1951. (MLS collection)

A rare view of the hoppers diverted away from their normal booked route via Disley Tunnel and Cheadle Heath. Here we see No. 48605 crossing the River Mersey at Heaton Mersey West Junction. The train will shortly regain its booked route at Cheadle Junction. Taken on 15 July 1951. (T. Lewis/MLS collection)

No. 48340 makes a spirited departure from Cheadle Heath and starts the long climb to the summit at Peak Forest, just over 16 miles away. All that remains at Cheadle Heath is a single line passing almost unnoticed behind the suburbs of Stockport. Taken on 28 July 1951. (B. K. B. Green/MLS collection)

Climbing up the 1 in 203, and into Ashley station with loaded hoppers, is Class 8F No. 48667. After a brief level section and descent, the climb resumes towards Knutsford. Still very much a rural station, Ashley has retained the former station building on the Manchester platform (now a private residence) and waiting shelter on the Chester platform side. Taken *c.* 1952. (G. M. Shoults/MLS collection)

No. 48613 gives assistance to classmate No. 48315, which appears to have expired en route back to Tunstead. The pair are seen climbing up the bank towards Chinley North Junction with a rake of nineteen empty hoppers with a brake van – note the new second wagon, recently delivered from Charles Roberts. Taken *c.* 1952. (G. M. Shoults/ MLS collection)

Passing through the station at Cheadle, on the former CLC line, is No. 48711. Originally opened by the CLC as Cheadle, but later renamed as Cheadle North by British Railways, on 1 July 1950, it lasted until closure at the end of November 1964, just short of its centenary year in 1966. Taken on 4 July 1953. (A. C. Gilbert/MLS collection)

During the winter of 1953/1954 essential work took place to repair Dove Holes tunnel due to the poor condition of the brick linings and severe water ingress. The hopper trains were diverted to run via Buxton and the LNWR line to Hazel Grove. No. 48613 is seen leaving New Mills Newtown station on one such working with loaded hoppers. Taken c. 1953. (N. Harrop/MLS collection)

A little further down the LNWR line towards Disley we see No. 48426 on a Sunday diversion, heading back up the 'Wessie' line to Buxton with empty hoppers. The nature of the chemical production at Northwich demanded that the flow of limestone could not be interrupted for long. Taken on 6 February 1954. (N. Harrop/MLS collection)

A wonderful view of the I. C. I. Tunstead quarry, taken from the east side of Great Rocks Dale. A Class 8F has just departed with another rake of loaded hoppers for Northwich. Further hoppers can be seen under the main loader along with a long rake of vans. The Derby to Manchester main line is in front of the departing hopper train. Taken *c.* 1955. (Courtesy of Brunner Mond Archive)

No. 48506 has been routed on the Down slow at Chinley with loaded hoppers, whilst Class 4F No. 44241 plods along on the Down fast with a coal and mixed goods train. It is possible for the hoppers to be switched to the Down fast either at Chinley Station North, Buxworth Junction, or New Mills South Junction, further down the line. Taken *c.* 1955. (M. Enefer courtesy of Barry Knapper collection)

Approaching Stoney Bridge at Timperley is No. 48254 with the Down hoppers. The train will shortly pass Skelton Junction and may be held on the curve for a clear path towards Hale up the short, steep and curved Hale Bank. Taken *c.* 1955. (Collection of B. K. B. Green)

Rolling down through Hazel Grove when it was just fields, No. 48045 approaches Rutter's Lane bridge. The fields off to the left are all now part of the Newby Road Industrial Estate between the LNWR and MR lines. In the 1930s a proposal was put forward to link the Midland with the LNWR lines crossing these fields. Alas, it was never built, but a chord line was opened in 1986 where the lines cross over at Hazel Grove itself. Taken *c.* 1955. (R. Keeley/MLS collection)

Rounding the curve and past Chinley North Junction signalbox is No. 48045, with the driver keeping a watchful eye on the photographer. Nowadays, Chinley North Junction is still a busy location with TransPennine Express, local passenger services, freight to and from the Peak Forest area and Earles Sidings at Hope. Taken *c.* 1956. (Collection of B.K.B. Green)

A low-level view of No. 48426 passing through Lostock Gralam station with a rake of empties. Lostock Gralam is located just to the east of Northwich on the former route of the Roman road Watling Street. For many years there was a goods yard, now all replaced by a secure storage site. The station is unmanned on the Mid-Cheshire line. Taken *c.* 1956. (W. D. Cooper/Gordon Coltas Photographic Trust)

Heading along the Up fast line, and just entering Buxworth Cutting, we see No. 48683 with empties for Tunstead. Part of the cutting was originally a tunnel, until this was opened out to allow the lines to be quadrupled to handle increased traffic. Now it is just back to double track, though a proposal to reinstate a third track for freight traffic has been suggested to give extra capacity. Taken *c.* 1956. (A. C. Gilbert/MLS collection)

Making steady progress for the climb up Hale Bank, No. 48711 heads under the 1,500 volt DC overhead wires of the Manchester, South Junction & Altrincham Railway (MSJ&AR). The Class 8F is just about to enter Altrincham station with the 2.5 p.m. loaded train from Tunstead to Wallerscote works. Taken on 22 April 1956. (R. Gee/MLS collection)

The small station at Baguley was squeezed in between two road overbridges at Shady Lane and Brooks Drive. No. 48045 is seen passing the Up station building with empty hoppers for Great Rocks sidings. Taken on 23 May 1956. (P. Hutchinson/MLS collection)

No. 48717 is seen working hard between Chinley station and North Junction on the Up fast line between Deansgate and Dakin's overbridges; the photographer is stood on Dakin's overbridge looking towards Chinley. Taken on 24 August 1956. (MLS collection)

In mid-January 1957, British Railways started trials with a then recently new Standard Class 9F locomotive, No. 92045, built at Crewe in 1955. Over a three-day period, the Bidston-based Class 9F was used and is seen here tackling Hale Bank on the final day with a loaded rake of nineteen hoppers. Taken on 15 January 1957. (A. W. Martin)

Passing the end of New Mills Goods yard is No. 48296 with Up empties for Great Rocks sidings. The locomotive is just passing over the points connecting the Heaton Mersey lines to the lines coming in from Marple, immediately becoming the fast and slow lines to and from Chinley North Junction. Taken on 1 June 1957. (MLS collection)

Once out of the suburbs of Altrincham and Hale the landscape changes to a more rural look. No. 48506 has just passed the station, level crossing and signalbox at Mobberley with a loaded train of hoppers. Mobberley signalbox still survives to this day to control the level crossing and signalling to/from Deansgate Junction and Plumley West boxes. Taken on 20 August 1957. (MLS collection)

In days gone by it was possible to obtain a British Railways lineside permit and take photographs of passing trains from the lineside, as shown here. No. 48135 heads back up to Great Rocks sidings with a train of empty hoppers on the Up fast at Buxworth Junction, as the photographer stands on the Down slow line. Taken on 20 June 1957. (MLS collection)

I. C. I. owned and operated a fleet of steam shunters at Tunstead to assist with train preparation. Avonside-built No. RS/1 is seen drawing loaded hopper wagons out from under the main loader with snow on the ground. Taken on 14 March 1958. (Courtesy of Tarmac Buxton Cement & Lime)

The driver will be keeping a check on the speed on the long descent down to Cheadle Junction as No. 48555 sweeps around the curve at Buxworth cutting with loaded hoppers for Northwich. This was the approximate location of the short tunnel that existed here, until it was opened out in 1900 to allow the two extra tracks to be built – these became the slow lines seen beyond the train. Taken on 5 July 1958. (W. A. Brown)

Having cleared the long descent from Peak Forest the locomotive crew will appreciate the gentle gradient down along the Mersey valley towards Northenden. No. 48605 is passing Cheadle West signalbox – a scene now long gone. Note the double-arm CLC lower quadrant shunting signal on the right-hand side. Taken on 8 April 1959. (MLS collection)

No. 48764 has just passed through the station and the east signalbox at Knutsford and coasts by with a train of empty hoppers, heading downhill towards Mobberley. Taken on 17 April 1960. (D. L. Chatfield/MLS collection)

Heading back towards Great Rocks sidings with a train of empty hopper wagons, No. 48764 enters the former station at Buxworth on the Up fast line. Bugsworth, as the station was known, until June 1930, became Buxworth and closed in September 1958. Taken on 18 June 1960. (MLS collection)

Standing at the head of the 10.30 a.m. empties is No. 48340, waiting for the photographer to climb on board the brake van at the rear on a hopper train ride to Tunstead and back. The location is Oakleigh sidings, the main yard for traffic in and out of I. C. I. Winnington works at Northwich. Taken on 9 July 1960. (A. C. Gilbert/MLS collection)

En route to Great Rocks sidings the train is seen, passing Chinley North Junction and the signalbox, from the brake van doorway at the rear of the train of fourteen hoppers. The usual load was sixteen wagons for a Class 8F like No. 48340. Taken on 9 July 1960. (W. A. Brown)

Having made his way down into the quarry sidings at Tunstead, photographer Alan Gilbert recorded another Class 8F, this time No. 48764 departing with another load of limestone for Northwich. Up to eight trains per day would run, serving the three works based around Northwich and so demand for the fresh stone was high. Taken on 9 July 1960. (A. C. Gilbert/MLS collection)

No. 48340 has been turned and watered at Great Rocks Junction and has arrived at the lower yard at Tunstead to collect the next rake of loaded hoppers, forming the 3.57 p.m. departure. Perhaps Alan Gilbert has captured his friends, including W. A. Brown, in the foreground, as the locomotive blows off steam. Taken on 9 July 1960. (A. C. Gilbert/MLS collection)

Working hard up the 1 in 90 with assistance from the banker at the rear, we see No. 48155 passing through Peak Forest on a fine August afternoon. Upper End overbridge is in the background – this bridge and the pipeline across the top are both long gone, having been demolished on 1 August 2004. Taken on 15 August 1960. (MLS collection)

On the other side of the summit at Peak Forest we see No. 48426 slogging up the last quarter mile or so until the summit of 985 feet (982.49 feet according to Midland Railway maps). The sheer sides of the limestone cutting leading to Dove Holes tunnel were all hewn out by navvies and the whole tunnel took around three years to build. Taken on 8 April 1961. (MLS collection)

Looking the other way, we see No. 48711 heading down with loaded hoppers. The driver and fireman will be keeping a check on their speed downhill, especially in the damp and wet Dove Holes tunnel ahead. Much remedial work has been carried out since it officially opened in 1865. Taken on 11 April 1961. (MLS collection)

Nine days later we catch up with No. 48711 as it restarts its train of empty hoppers from Cheadle Heath, as viewed from the railway footbridge. Note the L. M. C. R. A. railwaymen's club being built on the land beyond the fence. The club building still stands to this day. Taken on 20 April 1961. (P. Reeves/MLS collection)

On the same day we see No. 48017, crossing over Northenden Junction with the ex-LNWR lines from Stockport Edgeley, with a Down hopper train. Behind the photographer is Longley Lane bridge. The refuse transfer station now occupies the land on the far right. Taken on 20 April 1961. (P. Reeves/MLS collection)

Drifting into the Up Liverpool platform, having just passed under Stockport Road bridge, No. 48017 will stop at the signal to await a path to New Mills South. Like Chinley, the generously sized station and facilities provided at Cheadle Heath were intended to allow passengers to change trains here. Taken on 1 July 1961. (MLS collection)

Taken from the trackside of the ex-LNWR line to Buxton, No. 48693 is tackling the climb through Hazel Grove and is seen crossing over the large girder bridge where the two lines cross. The LNWR insisted on a four-track span and so the Midland Railway duly built the bridge, only for the LNWR line to remain double track. Taken on 25 November 1961. (J. W. Sutherland/MLS collection)

Rolling along on the Down fast line, No. 48605, and the train of loaded hoppers, has just passed through the former station at Buxworth. By now the Up fast platform had been removed, leaving only the station building and remains of the Down platform in situ. Taken c. 1961. (MLS collection)

The fireman leans out to see what the photographer is doing as No. 48340, on the Up fast line, climbs the bank past Gowhole yard. The Down marshalling sidings lay in the gap between the fast and slow lines, seen to the right of the locomotive. The Up marshalling sidings lay just to the north of the slow lines and are controlled by Gowhole Goods Junction signalbox. Taken c. 1961. (MLS collection)

This is the northern portal of Dove Holes tunnel and No. 48135 has just emerged back into the daylight, near Chapel-en-le-Frith, from the 1-mile 1,224-yard-long tunnel. The north-western end of the tunnel was of 'cut and cover' construction to replace the earlier troublesome cutting. Taken on 16 May 1962. (W. D. Cooper/ Gordon Coltas Photographic Trust)

In this lovely colour slide image, No. 48166 passes Cheadle Heath North signalbox and is about to pass under Stockport Road bridge and into Cheadle Heath station. In the background are the original post-war prefab houses on Hoylake Road and beyond the Gorsey Bank estate; they are now all long gone. Taken *c.* 1962. (MLS collection)

This photograph was taken from the balcony outside Bramhall Moor Lane Goods signalbox, near Hazel Grove. No. 48631 coasts downhill with loaded hoppers for Northwich. Note the lattice signal post just in front of the signalbox with an underslung arm for sighting purposes. Taken on 2 March 1963. (P. Martin)

With the regulator open, No. 48462 will need all the power available and a clear road to enable the short, steep Hale Bank to be climbed successfully. Metrolink trams and the railways now share Navigation Road station, each running on bi-directional single lines between here and just before the level crossing to Deansgate Junction nearby. Taken on 1 May 1963. (J. B. Arnold/MLS collection)

Restarting its train of empty hoppers, No. 48764 is seen departing the Up siding at Hazel Grove Midland and is crossing over Scarhill bridge No. 16. It was not uncommon to recess freight trains here, but the job would have been made easier if the siding had been made into a loop, like at Disley Goods. Taken on 26 April 1963. (P. Martin)

By 1963 thoughts had turned to trials using diesel-electric locomotives which would replace the Class 8Fs and 9Fs in the coming years. And so, in April 1963, these trials started, using English Electric Type 4 diesels (later Class 40). Here we see No. D228 *Samaria* on one such day, returning to Great Rocks sidings with empties through Hazel Grove. Taken on 26 April 1963. (P. Martin)

After the Type 4 trials it was then decided to try some Type 2 locomotives and the unique Metropolitan-Vickers diesel-electrics made an appearance from May 1963. The 'Co-Bos' as they became known, due to their wheel and bogie arrangements, were tried out singly and in pairs, as seen here as Nos D5711 and D5714 approach Altrincham station on one such working. Taken on 23 May 1963. (T. K. Widd)

No. D5714 is just passing the tall brick-built signalbox at Northenden Junction with an Up train of empty hoppers, heading back to Great Rocks sidings. The 'Co-Bos' were often seen as unreliable and prone to failures; this was mainly attributed to the two-stroke diesel engine not being able to cope with the cyclic demand of railway operations, the engine originally being developed for marine use in ships. Taken during May 1963. (Rail Photoprints Collection)

Swathed in a cloud of steam is No. 48605 at the rear of a rake of hopper wagons in Gorstage sidings (also known as Wallerscote sidings). These sidings were built in the early 1950s to serve the I. C. I. Wallerscote works. Trains of hoppers worked in from Tunstead; outbound traffic included bulk soda ash and liquid chemicals. No. 48605 will haul this train to Great Rocks sidings with the photographer taking a ride in the brake van. Taken on 25 May 1963. (D L Chatfield)

Looking ahead from the brake van, the train of empty hoppers hauled by No. 48605 has been brought to a stand on the 'Liverpool curve' at Cheadle Heath. In the opposite direction No. 48693 approaches from Tunstead and will draw up to the home signal, seen in the foreground. In the 1950s and 1960s it was possible for eight return hopper trains to run each day. Taken on 25 May 1963. (D. L. Chatfield)

The main Down line signal is on and so the engine crew of No. 48155 will ease out of the bottom sidings at Tunstead, with a banker on the rear. Once their signal is pulled off it will be ready to build up speed to climb to the summit just after Peak Forest North. Note the enamel wagon number plate affixed to the solebar of No. 3248. Taken on 25 May 1963. (D. L. Chatfield/MLS collection)

No. 48254, again in colour, this time crossing over at Chinley North Junction with a fourteen-wagon and brake van load for Great Rocks sidings. In the 1950s and 1960s many Class 8Fs relinquished their Stanier tenders in exchange for Fowler tenders. Taken on 13 July 1963. (B. Swainston/Author's collection)

Having tried both Type 4 and Type 2 diesel-electric locomotives in May, a further trial using the 'Co-Bos' took place in September, and then again in early 1964. Here we see No. D5719 passing Hazel Grove Midland with a rake of empty hoppers. 'Co-Bos' Nos D5700/03/07/08/11/13/14/17/19 are known to have hauled the hopper trains. Taken on 12 September 1963. (P. Martin)

Heading the 12.40 p.m. train from Tunstead is No. 48717, entering Altrincham station and passing the former CLC lower quadrant home signal with shunting arm below. Beyond the train is the goods yard, now home to a car park and leisure centre. Taken on 17 May 1964. (J. B. Arnold/MLS collection)

The thirty-seven-chain-long Liverpool curve was built by the Midland Railway to link between the Midland line to Manchester Central and the lower C. L. C. Godley to Glazebrook line. No. 48135 approaches Cheadle Junction with the Down hoppers to Northwich. Taken on 16 July 1964. (J. W. Sutherland/MLS collection)

Taken from almost the same position as the Class 8Fs photographed years earlier, we see No. D5278 overtaking 'Black 5' No. 45083, seen over on the Up slow line, near New Mills South Junction. Sadly, No. D5278 only had a short working career with British Railways. The locomotive was withdrawn after severe accident damage sustained in a collision near Peak Forest in January 1971. This locomotive was the first of the class to be withdrawn, in May 1971. It was cut up by October the same year. Taken *c.* 1965. (A. H. Bryant/Rail Photoprints)

In this undated view, one of the Trafford Park-allocated Type 2s is seen approaching Great Rocks Junction signalbox. The diesel was being banked on the climb up to the summit by a Buxton-based Class 8F at the rear. The Type 2s performed well on these duties until around 1984. The diesels were able to handle eighteen loaded wagons, two more than the Class 8Fs. Taken *c.* 1965. (Author's collection)

The hillside of Cracken Edge rises above. No. D5275 is seen with a rake of eighteen empty hoppers and a brake van at Deansgate overbridge on the approach to Chinley North Junction. Note that the eighth wagon has recently been outshopped from the I. C. I. works at Avenue, at Northwich. Taken on 6 October 1965. (J. W. Sutherland/MLS collection)

After the diesel Type 2s took over, the main role of the Class 8Fs was to bank the trains from Tunstead up to Peak Forest summit. Here, No. 48465 is seen doing its duty on one such train. Type 2 No. D5276 is out of sight at the front as the train passes through Peak Forest station. The station name had changed four months previously, from Peak Forest for Peak Dale, and would close fully in March 1967. Taken on 6 October 1965. (J. W. Sutherland/MLS collection)

Class 8Fs were the motive power called on to cover for failures and non-availability of the Type 2s after 1964. Here, on one such occasion, No. 48334 is seen passing the signal box at Knutsford West with Down hoppers for Northwich. Taken on 15 March 1966. (D. L. Chatfield/MLS collection)

Passing the signalbox at Peak Forest North is No. 48741 with the 15.15 ex-Northwich Up hoppers. The box survived until closure in August 1968 and much of the trackwork was swept away, with just the main lines and two sidings beyond remaining to the present day. Beyond is the Holderness quarry, now part of a much expanded Cemex Dove Holes quarry. Taken on 18 June 1966. (G. Neve/MLS collection)

On one of the few occasions that Class 9Fs were rostered to work the hoppers we see No. 92082 rounding the curve and under the 'Black Bridge' concrete footbridge, near Timperley. Most freight work around Northwich did not usually warrant the power of a Class 9F, so the hopper trains did not tax these locomotives unduly. An ex-Crosti Class 9F, No. 92023, is known to have worked a train of hoppers in lieu of a failed diesel locomotive, believed to be from Skelton Junction to Northwich only. Taken on 24 September 1966. (Courtesy of TOPticl Digital Memories)

It is well known that many railway photographers packed up their cameras once steam working on British Rail declined and, consequently, everyday scenes with diesels were often overlooked. In this spring view at Stoney Bridge, Timperley, work-stained Type 2 No. D7617 passes the houses on Oakleigh Avenue and Park Drive that back onto the railway. Seventeen empty hoppers and a brake van are in tow behind the locomotive. Taken during April 1968. (MLS collection)

Another view of Tunstead, this time from June 1970, where a Class 25 is seen departing with another load of hoppers. Compared to the earlier view from the 1950s, the trench that existed between the lines has nearly been filled in and there are a lot more newer quarry buildings on the horizon now. The main line is still double-track but will soon be singled between Great Rocks Junction and Buxton. Taken in June 1970. (Courtesy of Brunner Mond Archive)

Showing the head code '6F42' we see a green-liveried Class 25 on Down hoppers passing Bridge Hall, Adswood, and what was then the Simon-Carves and National Oilwell engineering sites. The track has recently been ballasted, as viewed from the LNWR line overbridge. A new road overbridge was built over the line, in 1997, to serve the new police station and industrial units. Taken on 24 March 1973. (A. Steele)

Here the Down hoppers are seen running on the wrong line, following the derailment of a train of cement 'Presflo' wagons. The location is Hazel Grove Midland and Class 25 No. 7648 slowly passes the scene on the Down line. The poor condition of the track and bed was responsible for several derailments along this line after passenger services ceased in 1969. The p.way gang will be busy preparing to lay the new track down. Taken on 5 May 1973. (A. Steele)

The driver of No. 7652 has applied some power as a train of empties passes over the junction at Cheadle Junction, and onto the short 'Liverpool curve', as it was known, round to Cheadle Heath. Class 25s, from new, were booked to haul eighteen wagons on the trains to and from Northwich. The requirement for a brake van had now been dispensed with by this time. The I. C. I. PHV hoppers were fully vacuum-braked from new. Taken on 8 December 1973. (A. Steele)

Coming off the 'Liverpool curve', and past Cheadle Junction signalbox, is Class 40 No. 40105, with an afternoon service to Northwich, just catching the setting wintertime sunlight. Class 40s were common traction for the hoppers, operating alongside the Class 25s until around 1984. Taken on 8 December 1973. (A. Steele)

Taken from the window of Altrincham signalbox, a Class 25 is seen heading towards Deansgate Junction with empty hoppers. The pedestrians and cars wait for the train to pass and the gates to be swung open. In the background is the then new Woodlands Road bridge, which would hasten the closure of the level crossing. Taken during September 1974. (G. Neve/MLS collection)

Powering away from the junction and through the disused closed station at Northenden is No. 7545, with a loaded train of hoppers for Northwich. The station here closed in November 1964, along with Baguley and Cheadle stations on this stretch of line. Taken on 22 January 1974. (A. Steele)

A Class 25 is seen departing Northwich, passing Sandbach Junction signalbox and heading towards either Winnington or Wallerscote works, with a rake of loaded hoppers. The train will have paused in the yard to collect the banking engine – often another Class 25 or sometimes a Class 40 – before restarting to climb up over the River Weaver viaduct towards Greenbank and Hartford. Taken *c.* 1970s. (R. Avery)

A fine afternoon sees No. 25109, on full power, passing through Altrincham station as it prepares to start the short, steep bank of 1 in 132 up to Hale. The island platform was later extended and the old goods yard behind the station is now home to a car park and ice rink dome. Taken on 4 June 1976. (Author's collection)

Class 40 No. 40130 is today's banker at Northwich and has a clear road to run past the train of loaded hoppers hauled by No. 25116, seen behind. Once behind the train and buffered up to the rear hopper wagon, the signaller will set the road and pull off the signals to allow the train to depart towards Oakleigh sidings for I. C. I.'s Winnington works. Taken on 16 January 1977. (J. F. Ward collection of J. Suter)

No. 25105 enters the station platform at Guide Bridge with a Down loaded roadstone service to one of the terminals in north-east Manchester. Guide Bridge has changed a lot since this photograph was taken, but the siding that the ex-GWR push-pull coach is stabled on is still there. This coach had a special role when royalty visited the area in 1978. Taken on 8 September 1978. (R. Stubley)

Most of the I. C. I.-owned PHV hopper wagons seemed to always be fifty shades of rusty brown, but the wagons were given a full overhaul every seven years at the rolling stock workshops at Avenue, near to Wallerscote works. One recently overhauled wagon is seen parked in the yard at Tunstead, waiting to take another trip to Northwich. Taken during February 1980. (G. Drinkwater/MLS collection)

On 22 February 1980, a serious derailment took place just after New Mills South Junction and all bar two hopper wagons ended up either derailed, damaged or down the embankment. The day after, No. 25088 is seen taking the Romiley line with a diverted train of hoppers. The driver is about to receive instructions from the signaller stood on the foot crossing. Ahead of the locomotive you can see the piled up wagons blocking the line towards Cheadle. Taken on 23 February 1980. (A. Steele)

Down in the Goyt valley fields, looking up towards New Mills South Junction, you can see the full extent of the derailment with five hopper wagons toppled down the bank, with a sixth on its side. The breakdown crane is working hard to remove the damaged wagons and load them onto 'Lowmac' wagons. The Class 08 shunter will take the short train of 'Lowmacs', loaded with the damaged wagons, to Chinley goods yard. Taken on 23 February 1980. (A. Steele)

Having been dumped in the station yard at Chinley, the damaged hopper wagons, including No. 19046, remained there until the scrap gang arrived to cut them up after salvaging any parts that could be safely reused. In the background, No. 40170 passes the forlorn wagons with another load of limestone for Northwich. Taken on 4 March 1980. (A. Steele)

Double trouble as a pair of Class 25s, lovingly known as 'Rats' by rail enthusiasts, head through New Mills South Junction. Nos 25192 and 25150 only have a short rake of ten empty hopper wagons as they head back up to Great Rocks sidings. The Class 25s had, by this time, been working the hoppers for sixteen years. Taken on 15 December 1980. (A. Steele)

Most of the original station track layout was still extant at Chinley, in 1981, when Class 46 No. 46031 was caught passing on a roadstone service. Class 46s were not common on the hopper traffic but when they visited the Buxton area it was not unknown for them to be 'borrowed' for such duties, until they were recalled by their home depot or sent back down to South Wales on the Margam lime train. Chinley Station North signalbox would close in December 1981. Taken during March 1981. (A. Steele)

More hopper mishaps, this time at Hartford East Junction where a routine banking move went wrong and ended up pushing several wagons off the track. Two wagons were damaged beyond repair and the lucky ones were upended out of the way. Viewed from a passing DMU passenger train, two of the original batch of eighty-four wagons are seen upturned, pending removal and repair at the nearby Avenue workshops. Taken during August 1981. (T. Booth)

Unfortunately, this wagon is beyond repair and would soon be history. It is believed to have been scrapped on site. Incidents of this nature tended not to make the local newspapers and the author once spent an afternoon in Northwich library trying to track down any reports on this accident, but to no avail. The residents of John Brunner Crescent may have been rather surprised to see the wagons nearly in their gardens. Taken during August 1981. (T. Booth)

As we have seen earlier in the book, diversions of the hopper trains using the former LNWR line from Stockport to Buxton ran in the 1950s and this would be the main route when Dove Holes tunnel was closed for maintainance. Here we see a pair of Class 40s passing through Whaley Bridge station, taking empty hoppers back towards Great Rocks sidings via a double reversal at Buxton and Great Rocks Junction. Taken *c*. 1981. (G. Neve/MLS collection)

If the booked route from New Mills South Junction to Northenden Junction was closed then the alternative was to run via Romiley, Guide Bridge and Stockport. A Class 25 is seen passing through platform 2 at Stockport with one such train. Note the trio of Class 40s stabled in the middle road loops locally known as 'The Slums'. Taken *c.* 1982. (C. Pearson/Author's collection)

One of the more unusual locomotive lash-ups seen on diverted hoppers was this trio leaving Buxton station. No. 37016 leads Nos 25153 and 25133 with a loaded train for Northwich. The train would tackle the steeply graded ex-LNWR line to Stockport, where the locos would detach. The two Class 25s would continue to Northwich alone after reversal, whilst the Class 37 would return to Buxton depot light engine. Taken *c.* 1980s. (D. Homer/Author's collection)

The distant signal is on as a disc headcode-fitted Class 40 approaches Northenden Junction with an afternoon train of empty hoppers. Behind the train are the bridges of the M56 and the slip roads to Junction 3A. Taken *c.* 1980s. (MLS collection)

Double-headed Class 45 'Peak' locomotives were a rarity on the hoppers, even more so on Northwich Mond services. Here we see Nos 45001 and 45019, with a rake of hoppers from Northwich in tow, coming off the Denton branch from the Stockport direction. Exactly what caused the double-header and the diversion is unknown. Taken at Guide Bridge on 22 January 1982. (R. Stubley)

Rounding the curve off the ex-OA&GB line from Crowthorn Junction to Stockport Junction, Guide Bridge, is No. 47284 with a rake of empty roadstone hoppers from either Dean Lane or Collyhurst Street. Class 47s started to be used on the hopper trains during the early 1980s. Taken on 29 January 1982. (R. Stubley)

A trusty Class 25 has been sent to the aid of its Sulzer Class 47 cousin. No. 25051 has been coupled onto the front of No. 47193, which appears to have failed, just after the junction, on a loaded train of eighteen hoppers to Northwich. The Class 25 would have been sent wrong line from Cheadle Junction. The train is passing over Newtown Viaduct at New Mills. Taken on 10 April 1984. (Courtesy of www.britishrailwayphotographs.com)

New concrete signal cable troughing has been dropped next to the Down Romiley line as No. 45004 *Royal Irish Fusilier* passes New Mills South Junction with an empty roadstone train of hoppers. During the next few months the track layout would be altered and most of the semaphore signals replaced by resited multiple-aspect colour-light signals. Taken during May 1984. (Author's collection)

Class 37s were regular visitors to the Buxton area from the 1970s onwards but only really started working on the hoppers from the 1980s onwards, initially on the roadstone services. Here No. 37208 is seen passing on the goods lines, behind Ashburys station, with a loaded train to either Collyhurst Street or Dean Lane. Taken on 29 May 1984. (J. Davenport/MLS collection)

Having first been trialled way back in 1963, the Class 40 locomotives were well liked by the locomotive crews on the hopper workings. On the occasion of the last 'Forty'-hauled Northwich hoppers we see No. 40181, crossing Newtown Viaduct at New Mills, working wrong line in the weak afternoon sunlight. The line between New Mills South and Cheadle Junction at this time was being worked as a single-track freight-only line. Taken on 10 November 1984. (S. J. Broome)

A familiar view to many enthusiasts is this one taken from the footpath leading to the fields behind Peak Forest South signalbox. Nos 20133 and 20134 power past the box with a loaded roadstone train. Northwich or Mond trains were loaded with large clasts of limestone, whereas roadstone trains were loaded with much smaller grades of limestone that would be crushed to become aggregate. Taken on 24 May 1985. (A. Steele)

The sole remaining building at Chinley station looks rather forlorn as a pair of Class 20s, Nos 20075 and 20153, pass through with a rake of empty I. C. I. limestone hoppers for Great Rocks Junction. Only the Up and Down lines remain and the station has been reduced to just a wayside island platform and passenger footbridge. Initially, pairs of Class 20s operated with a brake van as the guard was not permitted to ride in the rear cab. Taken on 30 May 1985. (S. MacCrudden)

Chinley station again, and another pair of Class 20s pass, this time Nos 20077 and 20141, with a rake of empty ICI roadstone hoppers from Portwood. The brake van and lower height ex-British Steel hopper wagons in the formation suggests this was a Portwood roadstone service. On the outward trip the brake van was on the rear to allow the propelling move down to Portwood from Woodley Junction. As a result, on the return, the brake van is behind the locomotives, as shown. Taken on 30 May 1985. (S. MacCrudden)

Engineering work on the usual booked route to Northwich often saw the hopper trains diverted via Buxton and Stockport. Here a pair of Class 20s, led by No. 20165 with sister No. 20007, bring diverted empty hoppers through platform 1 at Stockport. Alterations to the line between New Mills and Cheadle, relating to the construction of the Hazel Grove chord line, were taking place. Taken on 15 June 1985. (S. MacCrudden)

During 1986, British Rail tried out a small batch of eight Class 20 locomotives in an attempt to improve the braking capability of the locomotives when operating in pairs. From April to around November, the eight locomotives were used on the hoppers. Here Nos 20305 and 20306 are seen passing New Mills South Junction signal box with Up roadstone empties. Taken on 16 April 1986. (S. J. Broome)

A chance encounter by photographer Anthony Steele at Portwood captured what was though to be the last roadstone train to use the Tilcon stone drops. Stockport town centre provides the backdrop to the pair of Class 37s, Nos 37223 and 37226, as they marshall the loaded PHV roadstone hopper wagons. A new stone unloading terminal opened up the line, at Bredbury, allowing the closure of the line to Portwood and the extention of the then M63 motorway, now part of the M60 orbital motorway, eastwards. Taken on 7 October 1986. (A. Steele)

After the trials with the Class 20/3s, British Rail decided to try a pair of newly refurbished Class 37/7s from November 1986 through to Spring 1987, and they performed much better, having a greater tractive effort. Nos 37796 and 37803 were loaned from Cardiff Canton depot for these trials. Here No. 37796 is working solo on Up Mond empties, passing New Mills South Junction signalbox. Note the brake van and the name 'Roger' written in the dust on the cab front. Taken on 9 December 1986. (S. J. Broome)

Climbing up the short but steep Hale Bank and into the station we see a pair of Class 37/5s, in the original Railfreight Grey, with red stripe livery. A batch of thirteen refurbished Class 37/5s were allocated for Buxton area freight traffic duties from early 1987, once they were released into traffic from Crewe Works. Taken during June 1987. (MLS collection)

The refurbished Class 37/5 locomotives soon settled down into their role hauling the hopper traffic as required. They tended to share the Northwich traffic with Class 47s and the roadstone traffic with pairs of Class 20s and 31s. Nos 37683 and 37686 are seen departing Collyhurst Street with roadstone empties, the driver taking the chance to have a sip of his brew. From Miles Platting, the four-track mainline drops away to the right down to Manchester Victoria station. Taken on 11 August 1987. (S. J. Broome)

A pair of Class 37/5s, led by No. 37678, traverse the Up loop next to platform 1 at Stockport with a loaded rake of diverted hoppers for Northwich. The train will cross over to the Up fast line and then take the Chester line towards Northenden Junction. Note that platform 1A bay is still in situ – it was later filled in. The Up loop later became the line for platform 0. Taken during October 1988. (MLS collection)

Another diversion at Stockport, this time we see a pair of Class 37s, now adorned with the Railfreight Construction sector livery, which suited the locomotives very nicely. Nos 37425 *Sir Robert McAlpine/Concrete Bob* and 37687 are seen at the head of a rake of loaded PHV hoppers in Stockport's platform 3, having been diverted via Buxton and Hazel Grove. Taken during August 1990. (MLS collection)

A light covering of snow does not impeed Class 47 No. 47325 as it passes Peak Forest on the way back to Great Rocks Junction with empty hoppers from Northwich. Empty wagons were stabled in the reception sidings, located just to the south of Great Rocks Junction signal box. These would be collected by the works diesel shunter and taken for reloading when required. Taken during winter 1990. (C. Harrison)

Chapel-en-le-Frith, on the ex-LNWR line from Stockport to Buxton, plays host to a rather unusual manouevre on a Sunday diversion. A pair of Class 31s, Nos 31180 and 31296, have just reversed the train of loaded hoppers back across the cross-over to gain the Up line so the train can proceed towards Furness Vale wrong line to bypass engineering works ahead. Class 31s were never renowned for their haulage capabilities so this was an interesting move. Taken on 21 April 1991. (S. J. Broome)

Climbing up the 1-in-90, from Tunstead towards the summit at Peak Forest, with a loaded roadstone train are Class 31s Nos 31327 and 31229. Class 31s were often used on the roadstone services, displacing the Class 20s, until themselves being replaced by the Class 37s. Reorganisation of the British Rail wagon coding system saw the I. C. I. hoppers re-coded from PHV to JGV and also a change of ownership to Buxton Lime Industries, following the divestment of the I. C. I. empire. Taken on 22 April 1991. (S. J. Broome)

Looking the other way from Upper End Bridge, we see Class 47 No. 47452 *Aycliffe* hard at work banking the Class 31-hauled roadstone train towards Peak Forest. Former express passenger electric train heat (ETH) fitted Class 47/4s became quite common on the hopper traffic and Buxton freight workings from around 1990. This locomotive was withdrawn only four months later. Taken on 22 April 1991. (S. J. Broome)

Railfreight livery overload as a Tunstead to Hindlow service departs the Down and Up through line loop at Great Rocks Junction with four locomotives at the helm. The two Class 31s, Nos 31229 and 31327, had been added on front of the booked train locos, Class 37s Nos 37677 and 37678. The Class 31s would be taken off at Buxton and the Class 37s would continue to Hindlow alone. This flow of limestone commenced in 1987 and continues to this day. Taken on 26 April 1991. (S. J. Broome)

'Whoa' comes the shout from the shunter, stood on the ground with his hands up in the air, as the driver of Nos 37425 *Sir Robert McAlpine/Concrete Bob* and 37686 sets back onto an empty rake of JGV hoppers in Lostock works. Of the three soda ash and chemicals plants that I. C. I. once operated, only Lostock still takes in limestone from Tunstead, Wallerscote having closed in 1984 and Winnington stopped receiving limestone in 2014. Taken during March 1992. (Author's collection)

In the early 1990s the Class 37s went through a period of single locomotive operation and reduced trailing load on the hopper services, by now only running to Northwich for the Brunner Mond (UK) Limited works at Lostock and Winnington, and the Hindlow works of Buxton Lime Industries, following the end of the roadstone services. Here we see No. 37416 approaching Hale with just eight loaded hoppers in tow. Taken during August 1992. (MLS collection)

In this lovely spring view we see No. 37688 *Great Rocks* climbing away from Buxton, with a loaded rake of twelve hoppers, over Spring Gardens viaduct. In the distance is Buxton No. 1 signalbox and the Up Relief sidings, also known as Donnahue sidings. This is where the train had reversed, having arrived from Tunstead, via Great Rocks Junction. The vacuum-braked JGVs only had months to run before being replaced by air-braked bogie KPA hoppers. Taken on 9 March 1993 (S. J. Broome)

On another fine March day, No. 37688 *Great Rocks* is seen rounding the curve at Harpur Hill with a load of limestone for Hindlow lime works. Limestone extraction at Hindlow ceased in 1987 and this flow started to keep the lime production line going. The locomotive was named at Hindlow on 23 June 1988. In 2019, the locomotive was restored into Trainload Construction livery and reunited with its *Great Rocks* nameplates. Taken on 26 March 1993. (S. J. Broome)

Under leaden and rain-soaked skies, a pair of Class 37s, Nos 37417 *Highland Region* and 37686, do battle with wet, slippery rails and the adverse gradient to haul the rake of twenty-four JGV hoppers towards the line summit, just beyond Peak Forest. Like the former ETH-fitted Class 47/4s seen previously, the ETH-fitted Class 37/4 locomotives started appearing displaced by 'Sprinterisation' of their passenger work. Taken on 12 September 1994. (Author)

A classic viewpoint with some fine vintage diesel locomotives and wagons approaching. Nos 37415 *Mt. Etna* and 37405 *Strathclyde Region* sweep round the curve from the line summit at Peak Forest, with a long rake of empty hoppers for Great Rocks sidings. Pairs of Class 37s were booked to haul twenty-four loaded hoppers but could haul many more empties back. Taken during May 1995. (MLS collection)

A location seen before in the steam era with a Class 8F on the front. Same wagons, same traffic, but now with a classic pair of Class 37/4s up front, passing through Buxworth cutting. Nos 37426 *Mt. Vesuvius* and 37419 (formerly *Mt. Pinatubo*) descend from Chinley on 7F50, the 16:30 from Tunstead, accompanied by that lovely rushing noise the hoppers made when moving at speed. Taken on 9 July 1995. (S. J. Broome)

The driver of this pair of Class 37s is not hanging around at Altrincham as No. 37426, unofficially named *Mt. Vesuvius*, leads classmate, No. 37108, with the Northwich hoppers through the station platform. Tinsley depot staff added the hand-painted 'Volcano' names to four of its Class 37/4 locomotives in the InterCity Mainline colour scheme. Taken during July 1995. (MLS collection)

Once the privatisation era crept up on the railways the original fleet of Buxton-allocated Class 37/5s gradually moved away. They were initially replaced by Class 37/0, 4s and 5s based in the North West, like Crewe diesel depot. After that, pretty much any livery could be seen on the hoppers. Here Railfreight Metals liveried No. 37520 leads an InterCity Mainline 37/4 classmate with loaded hoppers through Mobberley station. Taken during March 1996. (R. Avery)

Thunderbird 415 has been called on to rescue two classmates that ran into difficulties on the way back to Great Rocks sidings. No. 37415 leads the errant pairing of Nos 37509 and 37518 as they pass Hazel Grove in the cutting leading towards the 2-mile, 346-yard-long Disley tunnel. Taken on 12 August 1996. (Author)

One of my regular haunts in Hazel Grove was Overbridge No. 26, better known as Rutter's Lane bridge. It was here one sunny February afternoon that I waited for the hoppers. The train could be heard rolling down from Disley and the resplendent EW&S (English, Welsh & Scottish Railway Limited) pair, Nos 37051 *Merehead* and 37707, duly came in to view, affording this photograph. Taken on 18 February 1997. (Author)

Having left the confines of Disley tunnel a pair of Class 37s, in the then new EW&S maroon and gold livery, approach the footbridge, near Disley, which crosses the line. Nos 37707 and 37051 *Merehead* head back to Great Rocks sidings with empty hoppers for Tunstead. I can remember spying the yellow cab front of the Class 37 from over 3 miles away, at the Hazel Grove end of the tunnel, with my binoculars, the tunnel being a straight bore. Taken on 3 March 1997. (Author)

Brunner Mond (UK) Limited owned and operated a small fleet of diesel-electric shunters for duties within its two works. On this occasion, Class 08 No. HL1007 (08867) has been hired in from RMS Locotec and is seen marshalling a rake of the JGV hoppers in the yard at Winnington; the first six wagons have been loaded with coke, whilst the seventh contains limestone. Many of the JGV wagons were relegated to internal use by 1997. Taken on 10 July 1997. (M. Saunders)

Later the same day, one of the Brunner Mond (UK) Limited diesel-electric shunters makes an appearance at Oakleigh sidings with a featherweight load of two empty JGVs, amounting to 46 tonnes or so. Five locomotives of a similar design to the BR Class 11 shunter were built by English Electric for I. C. I., in 1951, for use at Wallerscote and Winnington and all were named; this example was named *Perkin* after Sir William Henry Perkin, FRS. Taken on 10 July 1997. (M. Saunders)

The author's final view of the JGV hoppers in traffic was at Peak Forest one Sunday morning, where Class 37s Nos 37203 and 37220 crest the summit of the line with a rake of empties for Great Rocks sidings. The final loaded working using the JGV hoppers ran on 28 December 1997, behind Nos 37350 and 37380. The final set of empty hoppers returned to Great Rocks on 30 December, bringing an end to the reign of the former I. C. I. vacuum-braked hopper wagons on the mainline. Taken on 14 December 1997. (Author)

Once the JGV vacuum-braked hoppers had been retired, the traffic passed to a motley collection of two-axle PGA air-braked hopper wagons that were owned by CAIB and hired in by Brunner Mond for two years. Towards the end of November 1997, a trial had taken place using a rake of PGA hoppers to check they could be loaded and unloaded satisfactorily at each end. Here we see Nos 37245 and 37074 heading through Hazel Grove with a rake of PGA empties for Great Rocks sidings. Taken on 25 April 1998. (Author)

The PGA wagons were originally constructed by Procor in Wakefield in the mid-1970s and were leased to Foster Yeoman and ARC (Amey Roadstone Construction). This photo shows the former blue/grey Yeoman and the mustard yellow ARC liveries well. Some attempt was made at painting out the company names, usually with a blue or grey panel, with a CAIB vinyl sticker added for good measure. This rake is passing Hazel Grove near the site of the former Midland Railway station and signalbox. Taken on 25 April 1998. (Author)

This could almost be a 'guess the location' photograph. It is in fact at Skelton Junction, near Timperley, and Class 37s Nos 37175 and 37023 are in charge of a rake of empty PGAs from Oakleigh sidings. The line ahead from Northenden to Hazel Grove is believed to have been blocked and so this train was instructed to keep the line clear. This meant reversing the rake of hoppers back onto the former Partington branch line to stable until the line ahead to Tunstead was clear again. Taken on 20 March 1998. (J. B. Arnold)

The driver of No. 37038 has just buffered up to the short rake of empty PGAs in Oakleigh sidings at Northwich. Once the shunter has coupled up and connected the air-pipes and the brake test has been completed, the pair of Class 37s will depart to Lostock to collect more empties. Initially, the PGAs were hauled by Class 60s or pairs of Class 37s (as required) throughout 1998 until the Class 60s took over the traffic. Taken on 31 October 1998. (Author)

The former Midland Railway cut-off line from New Mills to Heaton Mersey opened in 1902. It is now just a single freight-only line between Hazel Grove and Cheadle Heath, then onwards to Northenden. Coal sector liveried Class 60 No. 60091 *Quinag* heads towards the High Level Junction with a rake of PGA hoppers. On rare occasions the line is host to passenger excursisons and test trains. Taken on 8 November 1998. (Author)

At Hazel Grove the first of the class, No. 60001, enters the Down Cheadle loop with the afternoon PGA hoppers for Northwich. The quantity of PGAs, and thus limestone, needed at each works varied and usually loaded up to a maximum of thirty-six wagons, depending on requirements. The returning empties could be the same or well over fifty odd wagons in tow, as recorded on several occasions. Taken on 19 May 1999. (Author)

Although officially booked for Class 60 haulage, there was one known occasion when a Class 56 was used on the hoppers to Northwich and back. Taken in the late summer evening, EW&S-liveried No. 56105 is seen approaching the signal at Hazel Grove with the empties from Northwich. Class 59/2s were also used for a while in late 1999 into 2000. Taken on 23 July 1999. (Author)

A Freight Facilities Grant enabled new unloading facilities and trackwork to be installed at Winnington and Lostock works. A brand-new fleet of twenty-seven air-braked JEA hopper wagons were built by W. H. Davis. Here all three designs of wagons used on the limestone traffic can be seen in the yard at Winnington. Brunner Mond had extended the hire of the PGA fleet from CAIB for an extra year, in 2000, until the proposed new wagons and facilities were ready to start, in January 2001. Taken on 9 September 2000. (Author)

The high-capacity JEA wagons settled down into a twice-daily service, serving each works, and usually loaded to twenty-five wagons being hauled by a Class 60. Here, No. 60096 cruises into Hale station with an afternoon train for Northwich. On occasions, when a Class 60 was not available, a Class 66 could substitute with a reduced trailing load. A pair of Class 66s would be needed to haul the full twenty-five wagons. Taken on 6 July 2002. (Author)

Knutsford is still a major station on the Mid-Cheshire passenger line between Manchester and Chester. Freight trains are slotted in between the hourly passenger services with 'The Hoppers' being the longest-running flow alongside newer flows like refuse, biomass and cement. No. 60020 passes through the station with another trainload of limestone for Northwich. Taken on 14 September 2002. (R. Avery)

A light layer of snow and a blue winter sky make for a crisp winter scene for No. 60010, in the EW&S maroon and gold livery, as it hurries through Hazel Grove with the morning empties. The train is on the Up Hope Valley line, whilst the Down Hope Valley, from which the Down Cheadle loop diverges from the turnout, is in the foreground. Taken on 5 February 2003. (Author)

This Class 60, No. 60060, is still clinging proudly on to its Trainload Coal sector livery and markings and name, *James Watt*, as it arrives at the rural looking Mobberley. The long block section between Mobberley and Plumley West signalboxes would occasionally require trains to be held here on the signal, before being allowed to proceed onwards once the line ahead was clear. Taken on 5 May 2003. (R. Avery)

Passing under the large redundant overhead catenary gantry at Altrincham station is No. 60083 *Mountsorrel* with the Northwich hoppers. The Manchester South Junction & Altrincham Railway (MSJ&AR) suburban electrified railway operated at 1,500 volts DC, from 1930 until 1971, when it was converted to 25kV AC operation. The gantry was later removed along with the passenger foot crossing. Taken on 3 March 2004. (Author)

Rounding the curve on the approach to Hazel Grove station, with a Sunday diversion, is No. 60072 *Cairn Toul*, in faded Mainline Freight sector grey livery. Like the BR steam and diesel eras, the former LNWR line from Buxton to Stockport was the primary choice for diverting the hoppers. On this occasion the train had a Class 60 on the rear of the rake of seventeen loaded JEA hoppers. Taken on 7 March 2004. (Author)

A well-timed view of the morning empties crossing over the River Weaver Navigation viaduct at Northwich in this photograph taken from Hunt's Lock. No. 60085 *MINI – Pride of Oxford* is in charge of the empties from Oakleigh sidings (from Winnington works) to Great Rocks sidings. Although the sidings had long gone at Oakleigh, trains were still described as being to or from Oakleigh sidings in the railway timetables. Taken during May 2004. (R. Avery)

Winding its way through suburbia is No. 60074, in the plain Mainline sector grey livery, seen climbing up the gradient from Altrincham to Hale. This view was taken from the Lloyd Street overbridge long before the cinema and leisure complex was built that now obscures this vantage point. Taken on 16 April 2005. (Author)

Another hopper diversion, this time with a twist. The booked route from Hazel Grove to Peak Forest was blocked, due to flooding in Dove Holes tunnel, over Christmas 2005. This necessitated a double-reversal at Hazel Grove from the single line from Northenden, to the passenger line to Buxton, via the Chord line. Here, No. 60033 *Tees Steel Express* is decending the Chord line in the Boxing Day gloom with a rake of empty JEAs tailed by No. 60036 *GEFCO* to reverse in platform 2. Taken on 26 December 2005. (Author)

No. 60021 *Star of the East* bursts into view at Hazel Grove from the long cutting down from Disley tunnel. By now the JEA wagons were looking rather worn and the Brunner Mond crescent logo and initials were starting to fade under the dirt. The Brunner Mond Group was purchased by Tata Chemicals Limited during 2006. Taken on 30 September 2006. (Author)

For a short period, in 2007, the JEA fleet of wagons were withdrawn from traffic due to repeated problems with the wheelsets. To allow the defective and damaged wheelsets to be replaced, wagons were tripped to Crewe Electric Depot for attention. To allow the services to continue, EWS hired in a rake of HIA bogie hopper wagons from Freightliner Heavy Haul. Here, No. 60015 *Bow Fell* is seen at Northwich drawing a loaded train, for Lostock works, forward. Taken on 28 April 2007. (Author)

Crossing over the A6 Chapel bypass road is No. 60056 *William Beveridge* with the morning empties from Northwich. The Class 60 has been adorned with the interim EWS 'Three Beasties' vinyl logo to replace the original Transrail logo. This was an attempt by EWS to standardise the appearance of their freight locomotives. Taken on 14 September 2007. (Author)

The haulage capabilities of the BR/Brush Class 60 locomotives are well documented and they handled the 2,500-tonne hopper trains with ease. No. 60089 *The Railway Horse* makes a fine sight accelerating through Peak Forest with the afternoon hoppers for Northwich. Eleven trains per week were booked to operate but it was not uncommon for weekday afternoon services to be cancelled. Taken on 20 October 2007. (Author)

In a rather tree-filled cutting, leading down from Disley tunnel, we see No. 60009 heading towards Hazel Grove. The photograph is taken from the footbridge that crosses the line here. In the background is Threaphurst Lane overbridge, then the western portal of Disley tunnel. Taken on 7 June 2008. (Author)

The overbridge that used to cross the line between Great Rocks and Peak Forest is no more. Known as Upper End overbridge, it used to carry a slurry pipeline across the tracks, and for many years the bridge was fenced off until it was demolished in August 2004. No. 60059 *Swinden Dalesman*, with faded Loadhaul logos, climbs up the gradient with the afternoon JEA hoppers. Taken on 3 July 2008. (Author)

Fast-forwarding the years to 2018 and the hopper traffic continued as always, despite the loss of Winnington works in February 2014. Freightliner took over the hoppers to Lostock works from the end of 2017 into mid-2018. DB Cargo (formerly EWS) were unable to provide sufficient traincrew cover at the time. The JEA wagons, now owned by DB Cargo, were used elsewhere on glass cullet traffic. No. 66622 is seen, battling through the snow flurries at Northwich station, with the morning train from Tunstead, formed of HIA hoppers. Taken on 27 February 2018. (Author)

Some classic motive power on display at Peak Forest, during the summer of 2018, as No. 60062 passes with the empty hoppers to Tunstead sidings. After DB Cargo resumed operating 'The Hoppers' in June 2018, they changed the diagram to start from Warrington Arpley yard instead of Peak Forest. Over on the right is No. 37716, shunting bogie box wagons in the Cemex quarry sidings whilst on hire from DRS to Victa Railfreight. Taken on 20 July 2018. (R. Avery)

A late afternoon stop-off, at Lostock Gralam station, between passenger trains afforded this photograph of No. 60010 with the 16:40 Tunstead sidings to Lostock works, supplying limestone for Tata Chemicals Europe. Lostock is now the sole remaining soda ash plant in Northwich and usually takes upto five trainloads per week. Taken on 29 March 2019. (Author)

No. 60010 has easily climbed up Hale Bank, and into the station platform, with the twenty-four loaded hoppers from Tunstead sidings. However, the section ahead to Mobberley is still occupied by the preceding passenger train to Chester, so the hoppers will have to wait at the signal until the section ahead is clear. The level crossing barriers will be lowered before the signal is cleared and the Class 60 restarts the heavy train, which was impressive to see and hear. Taken on 12 April 2019. (Author)

Approaching Stoney Bridge, near Timperley, on a drizzly Tuesday afternoon, we see No. 60010, again in charge of the 16:40 from Tunstead sidings. The allocated Class 60 often stays on this turn for several weeks at a time now the diagram has been altered to start from Warrington Arpley yard in the morning, and return there late night. Taken on 16 April 2019. (Author)

On arrival at Northwich TC (Terminal Complex), the loaded hopper train draws to a stand to wait for the shunter person to arrive, before obtaining permission from Greenbank signalbox to draw the train forward. Once the rear wagon is clear of the point this is changed over by the shunter. Class 60 No. 60040 *The Territorial Army Centenary* is seen drawing the hoppers forward, before setting back in to the works. Taken on 28 June 2019. (Author)

A major upgrade to Acton Grange Junction, just south of Warrington, at the end of July 2019 forced a change to the hopper services. For two weeks the diagram was changed to a morning light engine move, from Peak Forest to Lostock works, to collect the wagons, take them to Tunstead to be loaded then returned to Lostock, where all or some of the wagons would be discharged. The Class 60 then returned back to Peak Forest late at night. No. 60040 *The Territorial Army Centenary* is seen passing Plumley with the late-running empties to Tunstead. Taken on 26 July 2019. (Author)

Acknowledgements

The author and publisher would like to thank the following people/organisations for permission to use copyright material in this book: firstly, the Manchester Locomotive Society (MLS) has been a huge help in providing photos from the numerous collections that they hold – thanks must go to Paul Shackcloth and Chris Tasker in allowing me access to the collections and arranging scanning of their photographs and negatives; Trevor Moseley for information and his assistance; Frank Emerson from Tarmac Buxton Cement & Lime for permission to use photos from the archives at Tunstead; Eddie Johnson for access to the Gordon Coltas Trust Collection; Brian (B. K. B.) Green for photographs from his collection; Judith Wilde, formerly of Brunner Mond UK Limited, for permission to use photos from the Northwich archives; Barry Knapper for the Michael Enefer photograph from his collection; Tony (A. W.) Martin; W. A. Brown; David (D. L.) Chatfield; Peter Cross for putting me in touch with Peter Martin and his photos; Ken (T. K.) Widd; John Chalcraft for the A. H. Bryant and Rail Photoprints Collection photos; TOPticl Digital Memories; Anthony Steele; Bob Avery; Jeremy Suter for the John F. Ward photograph; Ron Stubley; Trevor Booth for his photographs and information; www.britishrailwayphotographs.com for permission to use their photograph; Stuart Broome; my uncle Stanley MacCrudden; my father Colin Harrison; and finally, Mark Saunders. Photographs from my own collection include those originally taken by Brian Swainston, Chris Pearson and Dave Homer.

Special thanks must go to Brian Arnold for his invaluable knowledge and photographs of 'The Hoppers' past and present.

Every attempt has been made to seek permission for copyright material used in this book. However, if we have inadvertently used copyright material without permission/ acknowledgement we apologise and we will make the necessary correction at the first opportunity.